W9-CPF-708

Four Town

WRITTEN BY NADIA HIGGINS • **ILLUSTRATED BY RONNIE ROONEY**

The Child's World

Published by The Child's World®
1980 Lookout Drive • Mankato, MN 56003-1705
800-599-READ • www.childsworld.com

ACKNOWLEDGMENTS
The Child's World®: Mary Berendes, Publishing Director
The Design Lab: Design and production
Red Line Editorial: Editorial direction

LIBRARY OF CONGRESS CATALOGING-IN-PUBLICATION DATA
Higgins, Nadia.
  Four town / written by Nadia Higgins ;
illustrated by Ronnie Rooney.
     p. cm.
  ISBN 978-1-60253-499-5 (lib. bd. : alk. paper)
1. Four (The number)—Juvenile literature. 2. Number concept—
Juvenile literature. I. Rooney, Ronnie, ill. II. Title. III. Title: 4 town.
  QA141.3.H574 2010
  513.2—dc22   2010007538

Printed in the United States of America in Mankato, Minnesota.
July 2010
F11538

About the Author

Nadia Higgins is a children's book writer in Minneapolis, Minnesota. She owns 1 wedding ring, 2 pairs of sneakers, and 7 plants. Her favorite time of day is 4 in the afternoon. That's when she gets to play Crazy Eights and other games with her 2 kids.

About the Illustrator

Ronnie Rooney was born and raised in Massachusetts. She attended the University of Massachusetts at Amherst for her undergraduate study and Savannah College of Art and Design for her MFA in illustration. Ronnie has illustrated numerous books for children. She hopes to pass this love of art on to her daughter.

four

The **4**s of **Four** Town adore the number **4**.

The silly **4**s love **four** so much that in winter they wear socks on their hands . . .

or mittens on their feet!
They love having **four** of a kind.

When it is really cold,
they put on **four** scarves!

Every morning, the **4**s
wake up at **four** o'clock.
They have so much to do!
They eat **four** breakfasts,

take **four** vitamins,

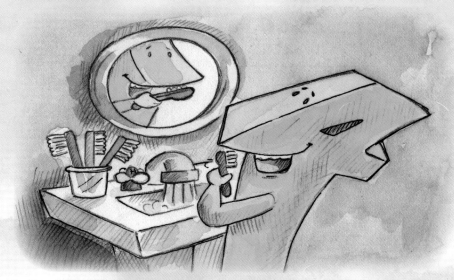

and brush their teeth **four** times.

Here comes the bus!

It's a quadruple-decker.

All the kids want the seats

on the fourth level.

Today is a special day
for the fourth graders.
They are going on a field trip
to the Museum of **Four**.

After school, Fiona **4** plays soccer.
There are **four 4**s on each team
and **four** soccer balls on the field.

At night, those **4**s pile up **four** pillows on their beds. It's time to rest their giant heads.

"Sleep tight, my little **4**."
Flo **4**'s Mom gives her **four**
kisses. "Tomorrow is another
four-tastic day!"

What Makes Four?

Cover two of the pictures with your hand.
How many are left?

Now try covering just one picture.
How many pictures remain uncovered?

How many pictures are left when you
cover three of the pictures?

Know Your Numbers

Hola, 4!

Do you know the number "four" in Spanish? It's cuatro. Say it: *KWA-tro.*

Favorite Shapes

4s have two favorite shapes. Can you guess what they are? Squares and rectangles. Each of these shapes has four sides and four corners.

Four Seasons

Why shouldn't you ever ask 4s what their favorite seasons are? Because they love spring, summer, fall, and winter all the same. The 4s are just so happy that four seasons make a year.

Four on Stage

The 4s are delighted to go see a quartet. That's four performers playing music together.

Woof!

What do 4s do when they pretend to be dogs? They "get down on all fours." That's an expression that means to get down on hands and knees.

Find Four

Can you find all the things that come in fours in this book? How many groups of four are there?